At Sylvan, we believe reading is one of life's most important and enriching abilities, and we're glad you've chosen our resources to help your child build these critically important skills. We know that the time you spend with your child reinforcing the lessons learned in school will contribute to his love of reading. This love of reading will translate into academic achievement. A successful reader is ready for the world around him, ready to do research, ready to experience the world of literature, and prepared to make the connections necessary to achieve in school and in life.

We use a research-based, step-by-step process in teaching reading at Sylvan that includes thought-provoking reading selections and activities. As students increase their success as readers they become more confident. With increasing confidence, students build even more success. Our Sylvan workbooks are designed to help you to help your child build the skills and confidence that will contribute to your child's success in school.

We're excited to partner with you to support the development of confident, well-prepared independent learners!

The Sylvan Team

D1472439

Sylvan Learning Center.
Unleash your child's potential here.

No matter how big or small the academic challenge, every child has the ability to learn. But sometimes children need help making it happen. Sylvan believes every child has the potential to do great things. And we know better than anyone else how to tap into that academic potential so that a child's future really is full of possibilities. Sylvan Learning Center is the place where your child can build and master the learning skills needed to succeed and unlock the potential you know is there.

The proven, personalized approach of our in-center programs deliver unparalleled results that other supplemental education services simply can't match. Your child's achievements will be seen not only in test scores and report cards but outside the classroom as well. And when he starts achieving his full potential, everyone will know it. You will see a new level of confidence come through in everything he does and every interaction he has.

How can Sylvan's personalized in-center approach help your child unleash his potential?

• Starting with our exclusive Sylvan Skills Assessment®, we pinpoint your child's exact academic needs.

• Then we develop a customized learning plan designed to achieve your child's academic goals.

• Through our method of skill mastery, your child will not only learn and master every skill in his personalized plan, he will be truly motivated and inspired to achieve his full potential.

To get started, simply contact your local Sylvan Learning Center to set up an appointment. And to learn more about Sylvan and our innovative in-center programs, call 1-800-EDUCATE or visit www.SylvanLearning.com. *With over 850 locations in North America, there is a Sylvan Learning Center near you!*

Kindergarten
Reading Readiness
Workbook

Published in the United States by Random House, Inc., New York, and in Canada by Random House of Canada Limited, Toronto.

www.sylvanlearning.com

Created by Smarterville Productions LLC
Producer: TJ Trochlil McGreevy
Producer & Editorial Direction: The Linguistic Edge
Writer: Erin Lassiter
Cover and Interior Illustrations: Duendes del Sur
Layout and Art Direction: SunDried Penguin
Art Manager: Adina Ficano

First Edition

ISBN: 978-0-375-43020-6

Library of Congress Cataloging-in-Publication Data available upon request.

This book is available at special discounts for bulk purchases for sales promotions or premiums. For more information, write to Special Markets/Premium Sales, 1745 Broadway, MD 6-2, New York, New York 10019 or e-mail specialmarkets@randomhouse.com.

PRINTED IN CHINA

10 9 8 7 6

Contents

Alphabet Zone

Alphabet Letter Search

The alphabet letters are playing hide and seek. CIRCLE each letter when you find it in the picture.

Ⓐ B C D E F G H I J K L M N O P Q R S T U V W X Y Z

Alphabet Maze

FOLLOW the path marked with **lowercase** letters to help the bunny go home.

Complete the Alphabet

FILL IN the chart with the missing letters.

Mm   Ww   Ss   Bb   Ff

Aa   Cc Dd Ee

Gg Hh Ii Jj Kk

Ll   Nn Oo Pp

Qq Rr   Tt Uu

Vv   Xx Yy Zz

Match the Letters

DRAW a line to connect the uppercase and lowercase letters that go together.

A   k

T   e

D   d

K   a

E   t

What's My Sound?

CIRCLE the pictures with the **m** sound.
COLOR the pictures for fun.

mitten

S s

What's My Sound?

DRAW lines from the "Ss" to pictures with the **s** sound. COLOR the pictures for fun.

Hide and Seek

LOOK at the farm. CIRCLE things that start with the **f** sound.

Ff

L l

2

What's My Sound?

CIRCLE the pictures with the l sound.
COLOR the pictures for fun.

What's My Sound?

DRAW lines from the "Rr" to pictures with the **r** sound.
COLOR the pictures for fun.

Rr

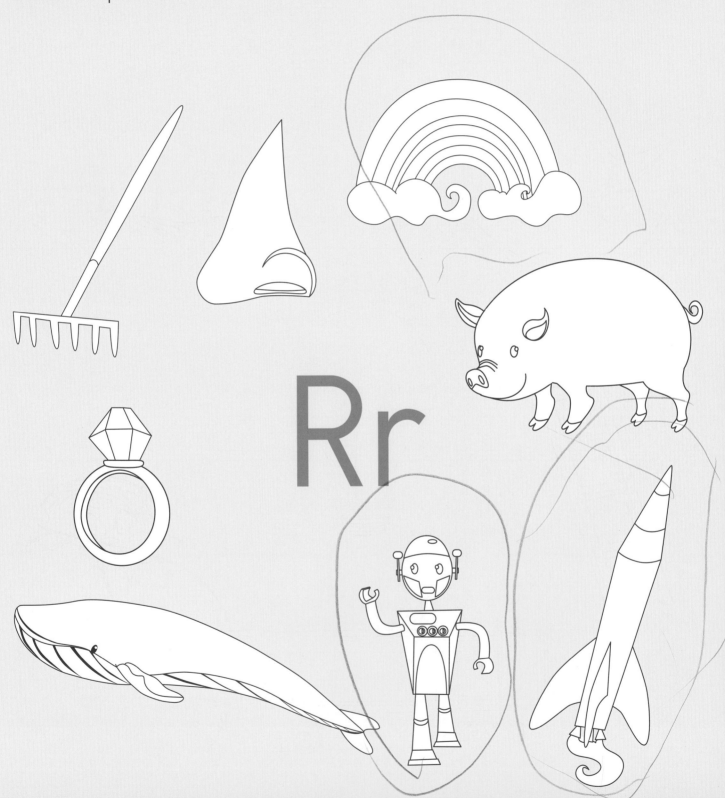

Rr

T t

Draw It

LOOK at the train. DRAW your own pictures with the **t** sound on the blank train cars.

Hide and Seek

Look at the park. CIRCLE the things and activities
in the park that start with the **p** sound.

Pp

Nn

What's My Sound?

DRAW lines from the "Nn" to pictures that start with the **n** sound. COLOR the pictures for fun.

Bb

Draw It

LOOK at the big bag. DRAW your own pictures with the **b** sound inside the big bag.

Cc

2

What's My Sound?

DRAW lines from the "Cc" to pictures with the **c** sound. COLOR the pictures for fun.

Hide and Seek

LOOK at the house. CIRCLE the things and activities
in the house that start with the **h** sound.

Gg

What's My Sound?

CIRCLE the pictures with the **g** sound.
COLOR the pictures for fun.

What's My Sound?

DRAW lines from the "Ww" to pictures that start with the **w** sound. COLOR the pictures for fun.

V v

What's My Sound?

CIRCLE the pictures that start with the v sound.
COLOR the pictures for fun.

What's My Sound?

CIRCLE the pictures that start with the **d** sound.
COLOR the pictures for fun.

Dd

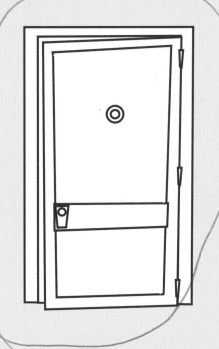

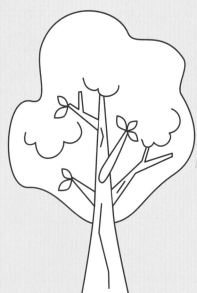

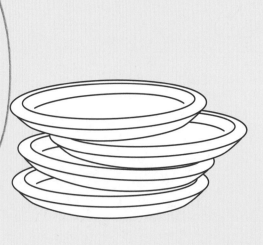

J j

What's My Sound?

DRAW lines from the "Jj" to pictures with the j sound. COLOR the pictures for fun.

J j

What's My Sound?

DRAW lines from the "Kk" to pictures that start with the k sound.
COLOR the pictures for fun.

Kk

Draw It

LOOK at the box. DRAW your own pictures with the **x** sound inside the box.

NOTE: Words that contain the sound but not the letter, such as **socks**, are okay.

What's My Sound?

CIRCLE the pictures that start with the y sound.
COLOR the pictures for fun.

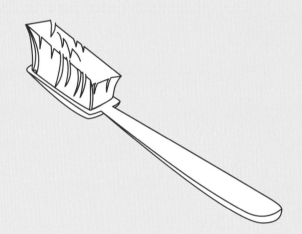

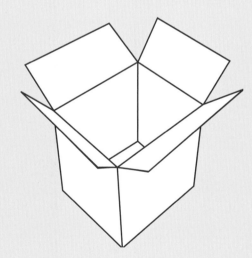

Zz

What's My Sound?

DRAW lines from the "Zz" to pictures that start with the **z** sound.
COLOR the pictures for fun.

ZOO

Zz

What's My Sound?

DRAW lines from the "qu" to pictures with the **qu** sound.
COLOR the pictures for fun.

qu

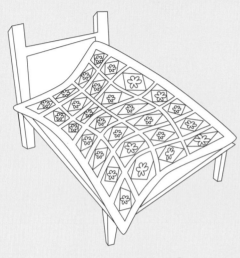

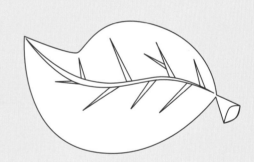

qu

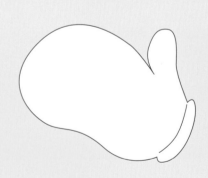

ck

What's My Sound?

DRAW lines from the "ck" to pictures with
the **ck** sound. COLOR the pictures for fun.

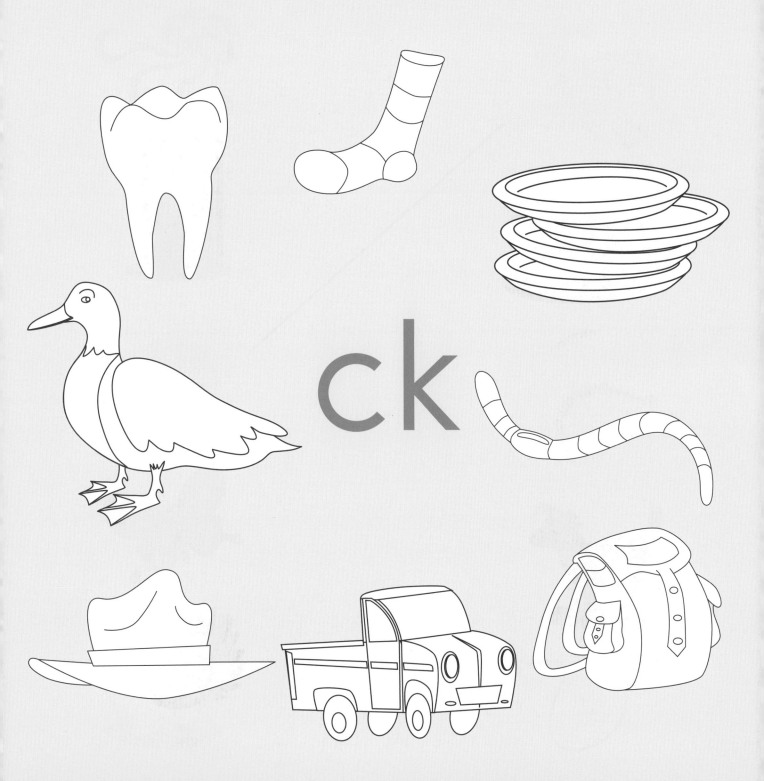

Beginning Sounds

Match Up

LOOK at the pictures. DRAW a line between the pictures that **begin** with the same sound.

Let's do some more!

Circle It

LOOK at the letter. CIRCLE the picture in the row that **begins** with the letter sound.

Hh

Nn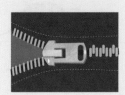

Rr

Ww

Starting Line

LOOK at the picture. WRITE the letter that makes the sound at the **beginning** of the word.

1   2   3

4   5   6

Match Up

LOOK at the pictures. DRAW a line between the pictures that **end** with the same sound.

Let's do some more!

Circle It

LOOK at the letter. CIRCLE the picture in the row that **ends** with the letter sound.

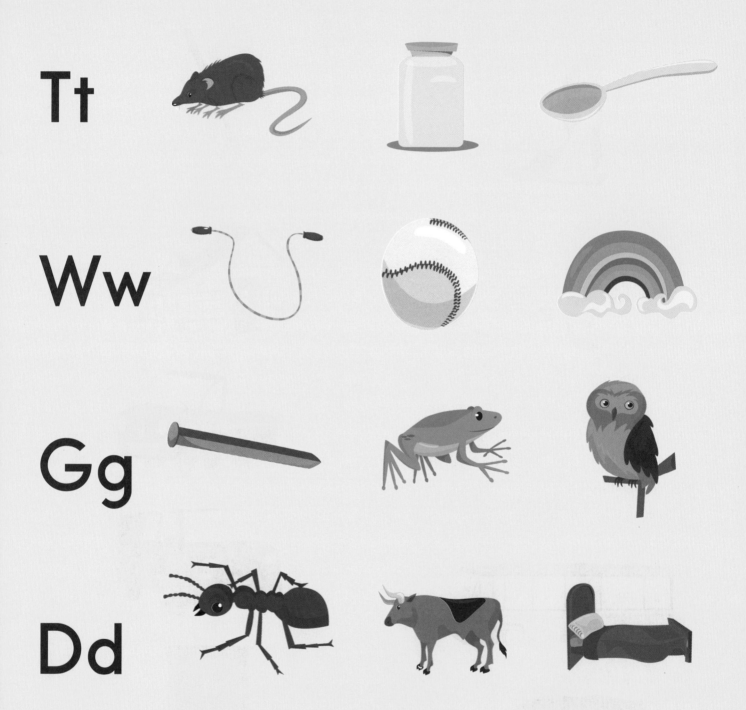

Tt

Ww

Gg

Dd

Finish Line

LOOK at the picture. WRITE the letter that makes the sound at the **end** of the word.

1

2

3

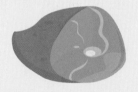

4

5

6

Match Up

DRAW a line between each letter and the picture with the same beginning sound.

M

F

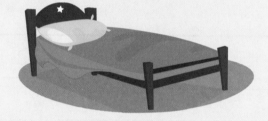

L

R

B

Let's do some more!

N

Z

Y

D

P

Starting Line

WRITE the letter or letters that make the **beginning** sound for each set of pictures.

Finish Line

WRITE the letter that makes the **ending** sound for each set of pictures.

_____
__ __ __
_____
1

_____
__ __ __
_____
2

_____
__ __ __
_____
3

_____
__ __ __
_____
4

_____
__ __ __
_____
5

What's My Sound?

DRAW lines from the "a" to pictures with the short **a** sound.
COLOR the pictures for fun.

a

a

What Am I?

MATCH the pictures to the words.

hat

pan

rat

bag

cat

What's My Sound?

DRAW lines from the "e" to pictures with the short **e** sound.
COLOR the pictures for fun.

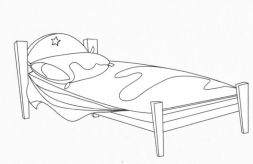

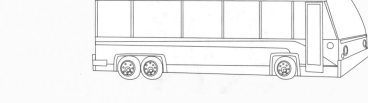

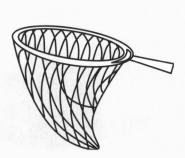

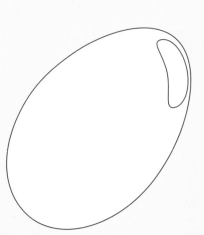

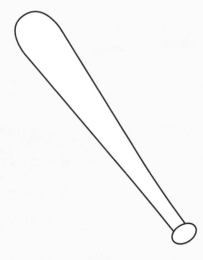

What Am I?

MATCH the pictures to the words.

web

hen

ten

net

bed

Short Vowels

What's My Sound?

DRAW lines from the "i" to pictures with the short i sound.
COLOR the pictures for fun.

i

What Am I?

MATCH the pictures to the words.

kick

bib

pig

sit

kid

What's My Sound?

DRAW lines from the "o" to pictures with the short **o** sound.
COLOR the pictures for fun.

What Am I?

MATCH the pictures to the words.

rod

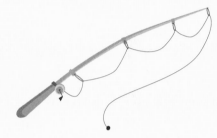

pot

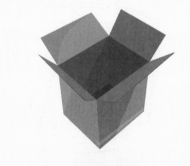

top

mop

box

What's My Sound?

DRAW lines from the "u" to pictures with the short **u** sound.
COLOR the pictures for fun.

U

u

What Am I?

MATCH the pictures to the words.

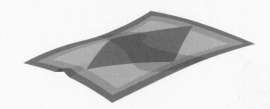 cup

 tub

 mud

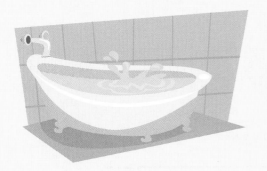 bug

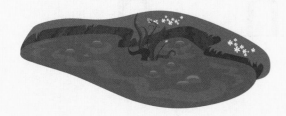 rug

Time to Rhyme

FILL IN the missing letter to make a rhyme to match the picture.

1
f   t   c   t

2
b   g   h   g

Match Up

MATCH the pictures that sound alike.

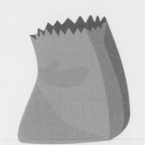

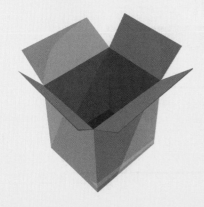

Time to Rhyme

FILL IN the missing letter to make a rhyme to match the picture.

1

m   n   r   n

2

f   n   r   n

Match Up

MATCH the pictures that sound alike.

Time to Rhyme

FILL IN the missing letter to make a rhyme that matches the picture.

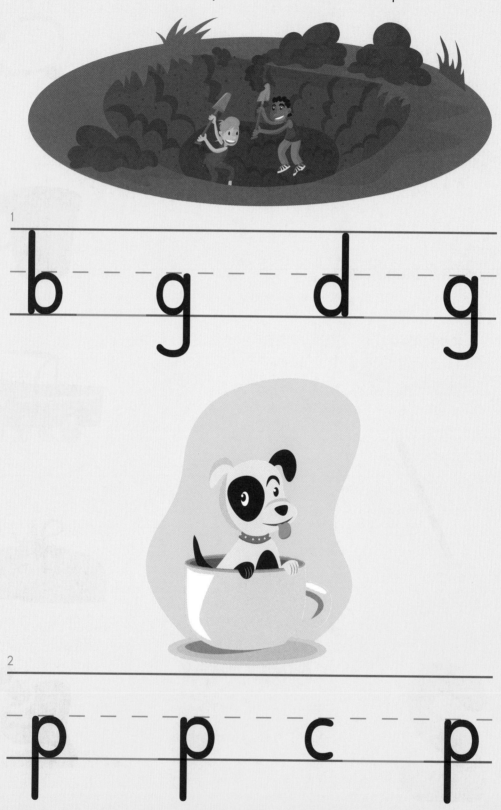

1

b   g   d   g

2

p   p   c   p

Match Up

MATCH the pictures that sound alike.

Time to Read

READ each sentence out loud. MATCH the sentences to the pictures.

I see the hat.

1. I see a man.

2. I see the rat.

3. I see a hen.

4. I see the bed.

Make a Book

DRAW a picture to match each sentence.

My Very Own Book
What Do I See?
Pictures by

_____

2

I see a cat.

4

I see a pan.

6

I see a jet.

8

I see a ham.

10

I see a bag.

Turn the page to finish your book.

Finish Your Book

CUT on the dotted lines. ASK a parent to staple the pages together. READ your book out loud. ✂

3

I see the hat.

1

I see the map.

7

I see the van.

5

I see the net.

11

I see the jam.

9

I see a bat.

Find the Missing Word

LOOK at each sentence. LOOK at the words in the word box. WRITE the correct word in each blank. CROSS OUT the words as you use them.

> **I**   **a**   ~~**see**~~   **jet**

1. I ___see___ the rat.

2. _____ see a man.

3. I see a _____.

4. I see _____ bed.

Time to Read

READ each sentence out loud. MATCH the sentences to the pictures.

1. I see a man
   and a cat.

2. The pig is wet.

3. I see a fox in
   a hat.

4. The rat is in
   the box.

Make a Book

DRAW a picture to match each sentence.

My Very Own Book
What Do I See?
Pictures by

_____

2

I see a man in a jet.

4

The ham is in the pan.

6

The cat is in the bed.

8

It is a big top.

10

It is a red dot.

Turn the page to finish your book.

More Words to Know

Finish Your Book

CUT on the dotted lines. ASK a parent to staple the pages together. READ your book out loud. ✂

3

I see a pig in a pen.

1

I see a kid and a pet.

7

The dog is in the van.

5

The rat is in the log.

11

It is a wet mop.

9

It is a hot pot.

Find the Missing Word

LOOK at each sentence. LOOK at the words in the word box. WRITE the correct word in each blank. CROSS OUT the words as you use them.

It   in   is   and

1. I see a cat _____ a dog.

2. The fox _____ red.

3. _____ is a big net.

4. The fan is _____ the den.

What's My Sound?

LOOK at the vowel. CIRCLE the picture with the same sound.

What's My Sound?

WRITE a letter to match the **middle** sound for each picture.

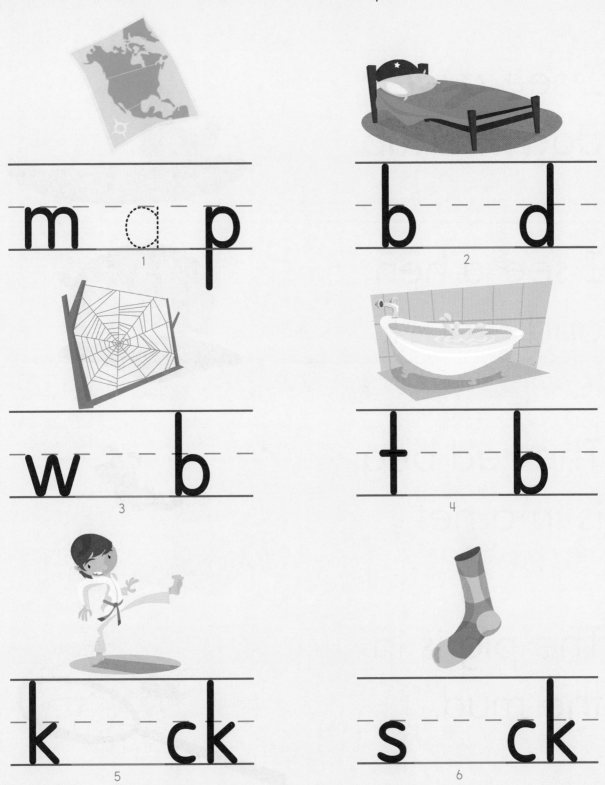

m a p
1

b   d
2

w   b
3

t   b
4

k   ck
5

s   ck
6

Match Up

READ each sentence out loud. MATCH the sentences to the pictures.

1. I see a wet dog in a tub.

2. I see a hen and a duck.

3. The red bug is in a net.

4. The pig is in the mud.

Find the Missing Word

LOOK at each sentence. LOOK at the words in the word box. WRITE the correct word in each blank.

| hot | It | and | The |

1. _____ box is big and red.

2. I see a pan _____ a can.

3. The sun is big and _____.

4. _____ is ham in a can.

Up and Down

Circle It

LOOK at the word. CIRCLE the picture that matches the word.

up    **down**

1. up

2. up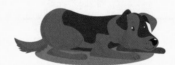

3. down

4. down

Which Way?

WRITE the word "up" or "down" to match the picture.

1. The jet is _____.

2. The man is _____.

3. The jet is _____.

4. The man is _____.

Time to Read

MATCH the sentences to the pictures. READ each sentence out loud.

1. Mom said, "Go to bed."

2. The van can go up.

3. I see you in the bus.

4. Liz said "sit" to the dog.

Make a Book

DRAW a picture to match each sentence.

My Very Own Book

The Story of Nan and Pat

Pictures by

_____

2

Pat had a rat.

4

Pat saw Nan.

6

Nan said, "Yes, you can pet the dog."

8

Pat said, "Yes, you can pet the rat."

10

Nan pet the rat.

Turn the page to finish your book.

Words to Know

Finish Your Book

CUT on the dotted lines. ASK a parent to staple the pages together. READ your book out loud. ✂

3

Nan saw Pat.

1

Nan had a dog.

7

Nan said, "Can I pet the rat?"

5

Pat said, "Can I pet the dog?"

11

The dog and the rat had a nap.

9

Pat pet the dog.

Find the Missing Word

LOOK at each sentence. LOOK at the words in the word box. WRITE the correct word in each blank. CROSS OUT the words as you use them.

said	go	to	down

1. You _____ up in the jet.

2. I sit _____ in the jet.

3. You _____, "It is fun."

4. The dog ran _____ the man.

Colors

Time to Read

LOOK at the color word. CIRCLE the picture that matches the color.

red   green   blue   yellow

1. red

2. green

3. blue

4. yellow

Make a Book

DRAW a picture to match each sentence.

My Very Own Book

Red, Green, Blue, and Yellow

Pictures by

_____

2

The sack is blue.

4

The sun is yellow.

6

The bed is blue.

8

The bug is yellow.

10

The bus is yellow.

Turn the page to finish your book.

Finish Your Book

CUT on the dotted lines. ASK a parent to staple the pages together. READ your book out loud. ✂

3

The cup is red.

1

The box is green.

7

The fox is red.

5

The sock is green.

11

The hat is red.

9

The jet is blue.

Draw It

READ each color word out loud. DRAW three things the same color inside each square.

yellow	red
blue	green

Circle It

LOOK at the word. CIRCLE the picture that matches the word.

big   **little**

1. big

2. little

3. big

4. little

Blank Out

WRITE the word "big" or "little" to match the picture.

1. The van is _____.

2. The egg is _____.

3. The top is _____.

4. The bed is _____.

Match Up

READ each sentence out loud. MATCH the sentences to the pictures.

1. I have a green box.

2. I have a yellow box for you.

3. The rat is on the big rug.

4. We have a blue sack.

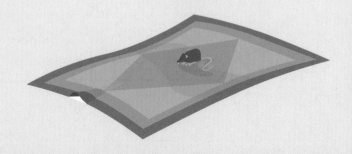

Make a Book

DRAW a picture to match each sentence.

My Very Own Book

A Dog, a Cat, and Hats

Pictures by

_____

2

We have a little cat.

4

The cat is on the rug.

6

We have a red hat for the cat.

8

We put the red hat on the cat.

10

We hug the cat.

Turn the page to finish your book.

Finish Your Book

CUT on the dotted lines. ASK a parent to staple the pages together. READ your book out loud. ✂

3

The dog is on the rug.

1

We have a big dog.

7

We put the blue hat on the dog.

5

We have a blue hat for the dog.

11

We have a dog and a cat in hats.

9

We hug the dog.

Find the Missing Word

LOOK at each sentence. LOOK at the words in the word box. WRITE the correct word in each blank. CROSS OUT the words as you use them.

for   **have**   **on**   **We**

1. We _____ a big van.

2. The mud is _____ the rug.

3. I have a job _____ you.

4. _____ see the yellow bus.

More Colors

Match Up

LOOK at the color word. CIRCLE the picture in the row that matches the color.

orange	purple	black	brown

1. orange

2. purple

3. black

4. brown

Make a Book

DRAW a picture to match each sentence.

My Very Own Book

Colors

Pictures by

_____

2

The bat is black.

4

The log is brown.

6

The rock is brown.

8

The mud is brown.

10

The pan is black.

Turn the page to finish your book.

Finish Your Book

CUT on the dotted lines. ASK a parent to staple the pages together. READ your book out loud. ✂

3

The rug is purple.

1

The cat is orange.

7

The jam is purple.

5

The van is orange.

11

The hat is purple.

9

The yam is orange.

Draw It

READ each color word out loud. DRAW three things the same color inside each square.

orange	purple
black	brown

Match Up

READ each sentence out loud. MATCH the sentences to the pictures.

1. We look at the map.

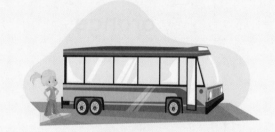

2. She is not on the bus.

3. He is not sad.

4. We look for a bug.

Draw the Story

READ the story out loud.

The Bus

I get on the bus. I see Sam. He is on the bus. I see Gus. He is on the bus. I see Pam. She is on the bus. We sit on the bus.

DRAW a picture to match the story.

Find the Missing Word

LOOK at each sentence. LOOK at the words in the word box. WRITE the correct word in each blank. CROSS OUT the words as you use them.

He	not	is	look

1. I _____ in the den for

the dog.

2. _____ is a big man.

3. The duck is _____ purple.

4. She _____ a brown hen.

Draw the Story

READ the story out loud.

The Pig

I have a pet pig. He is a little pig. He is a black pig. He is not a mad pig. He is not a sad pig. He is a fun pig.

DRAW a picture to match the story.

What Color Am I?

MATCH the color words to the pictures.

purple

yellow

orange

black

blue

Word Puzzles

CUT OUT the words. USE the words to create your own sentences.

The	the	the	I
and	see	have	go
You	you	a	a
She	she	is	can
He	he	to	for
little	on	in	big
duck	dog	cat	pig
bed	hat	rug	bug
bus	jet	yellow	brown
black	green	red	blue

Words I Know

LOOK at the words. READ each word out loud.

I	a	you	said
the	see	have	on
and	is	we	for
in	it	not	look
down	up	he	she
go	to	big	little

Story Characters

Who Is It?

The people and the animals in a story are the **characters**.

Animals

People

CIRCLE the pictures that can be characters in a story.

Who Is It?

READ the story out loud.

The Mud

The pig is in the mud. The dog is in the mud. The rat is in the mud. The hen is in the mud. The mud is brown. The mud is wet. It is fun.

CIRCLE the characters in the story.

Who Is It?

READ the story out loud.

The Mat

The duck ran to the man. The cat ran to the man. The duck sat on the mat. The cat sat on the mat. The man fed the duck and the cat on the mat.

CIRCLE the characters in the story.

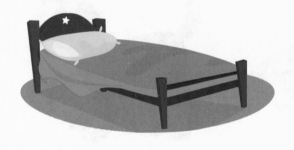

Who Is It?

READ the story out loud.

The Rat

A kid sat on a big rock. A dog sat on the rock. A cat sat on the rock. The kid said, "I see a rat." The cat ran. The dog ran. The kid ran.

DRAW the characters in the story.

Story Setting

Where Is It?

The place and time in a story create the **setting**.

Place

Time

CIRCLE the pictures that can be the setting for a story.

Where Is It?

READ the story out loud.

The Cat

I look for the cat. I look on the bed.
The cat is not on the bed. I look on
the rug. The cat is not on the rug. I
look in a big box. I see the cat. It is
in the big box.

CIRCLE the setting for the story.

Where Is It?

READ the story out loud.

The Run

He can run. She can run. I can run.
You can run. We run to the rock.
We run to the log. It is hot. We run
in the sun.

CIRCLE the setting for the story.

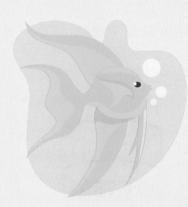

Where Is It?

READ the story out loud.

The Van

Dad is in the van. I get in the van. You get in the van. We look at the map. We go up. We go down. We go and go in the van.

DRAW the setting for the story.

What's the Order?

READ the story out loud.

Jam and Ham

I have a pot. I put ham in the pot. I put jam in the pot. I mix the ham and jam. Yum!

WRITE 1, 2, and 3 to show the beginning, middle, and end of the story.

_____   _____   _____

What's the Order?

A story has a beginning, a middle, and an end.

LOOK at the pictures. WRITE 1, 2, and 3 to show the correct order.

_____

_____

_____

_____

_____

_____

What's the Order?

READ the story out loud. DRAW the beginning, middle, and end of the story.

The Dog

I put the dog in the tub. I rub the dog. I put the dog in the sun.

1	2	3

What's the Order?

READ the story out loud. DRAW the beginning, middle, and end of the story.

The Cat Nap

I sit on the bed. I pat the cat.

I take a nap with the cat.

1	2	3

Story Problem and Solution

What's the Solution?

Most stories have a problem and a solution.

For example:

Problem	Solution

LOOK at the problem. DRAW the solution.

Problem	Solution

What's the Solution?

LOOK at the problem.

Problem

CIRCLE the correct solution to the problem.

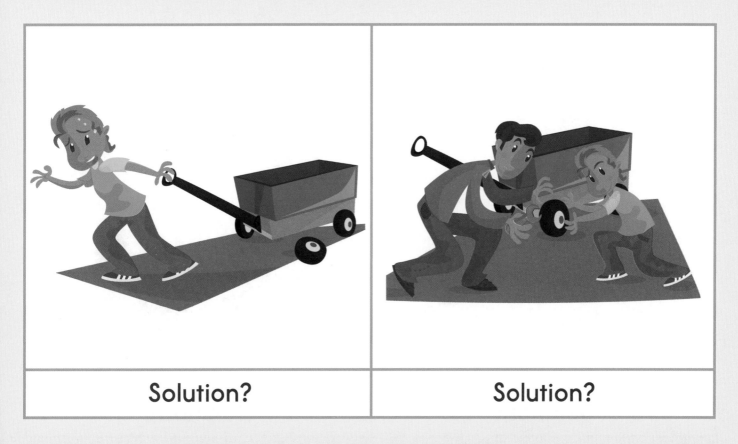

Solution?   Solution?

What's the Solution?

LOOK at the problem.

Problem

CIRCLE the correct solution to the problem.

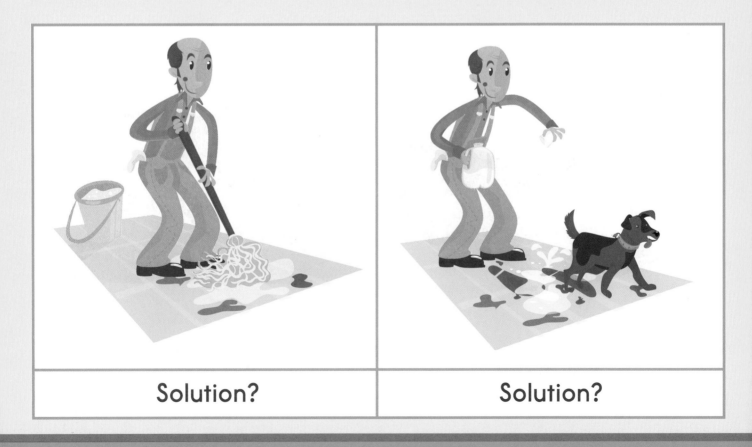

Solution?   Solution?

What's the Solution?

READ the story out loud.

> ## Ben
>
> Ben hid. I look in the den. Ben is not in the den. I look in the tub. I see Ben. He is in the tub.

DRAW the problem in the story. DRAW the solution in the story.

Problem	Solution

Draw the Story

READ the story out loud. DRAW a picture to answer each question about the story.

Meg

Meg is sick. She is in bed. She is sad. I have a dog. I go to see Meg. I put the dog on the bed. Meg can pet the dog on his back. The dog can lick Meg on the neck. Meg is sick. But she is not sad.

Who is it?

Where is it?

What is the problem?

What is the solution?

Draw the Story

READ the story out loud. DRAW what happens in the story in the correct order.

The Bug

A bug is on the pig. The pig is mad. I go to get a net. I get the bug in the net. I see a rock. I put the bug on the rock.

1	2

3	4

5	6

Who, Where, and What?

CIRCLE the picture that can be a character in a story.

CIRCLE the picture that can be the setting for a story.

CIRCLE the picture that can be a problem in a story.

What's the Story?

WRITE 1, 2, and 3, to show the beginning, middle, and end of the story.

CIRCLE the square that shows and tells the **problem** in the story.

I fan the dog in the sun.

_____

The dog is hot in the sun.

_____

I go get a fan.

_____

Answers

Page 2

Page 3

Page 4

1. Bb 2. Ff 3. Mm 4. Ss 5. Ww

Page 5

A — t
T — a
D — d
K — e
E — k

Page 6

mouse, moon, mitten, map, monkey

Page 7

sun, snail, stop, spoon, star

Page 8

fish, fence, frog, flies, flowers, farmer, face, fruit, flag, fan

Page 9

leaf, lightbulb, ladybug, ladder

Page 10

rainbow, rocket, robot, ring, rake

Page 11

Suggestions: tree, top, teeth, toothbrush, turkey, TV, table, toys, teacher, tea, tie, telephone

Page 12

police, play, path, picnic, pizza, piece of pizza, pie, purse, parrot, paint, painter, painting, person, puppy, post, picnic basket

Page 13

nose, net, nail, nine, nest

Page 14

Suggestions: bat, bug, boy, bread, butter, bottle, bone, bowl, button, bow, balloon, banana, belt

Page 15

car, carrot, corn, cake, cow

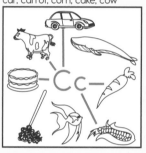

Page 16

ham, horse, hat, hang, hanger, hammer, heart, hair, hat stand, hands

Page 17

glasses, girl, goat, grapes

Page 18

whale, wagon, walrus, worm, window

Page 19

volcano, violin, van, vegetables

Page 20

door, dress, dishes, doll

Page 21

juice box, jar, jellyfish, jump rope

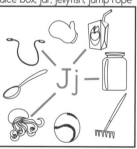

Answers

Page 22
kitten, kangaroo, kick, key

Page 23
Suggestions (can contain letter or sound): ox, taxi, fox, box, ax, six, rocks, socks, trucks, ducks, names with the x sound like Max or Rex

Page 24
yarn, yo-yo

Page 25
zebra, zipper, zoo

Page 26
quilt, question mark, queen

Page 27
sock, backpack, truck, duck

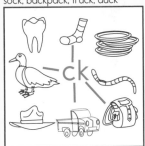

Page 28

Page 29

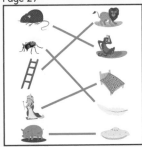

Page 30

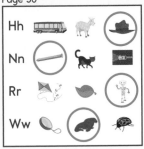

Page 31
1. m, 2. c (or k), 3. b, 4. d, 5. s, 6. l

Page 32

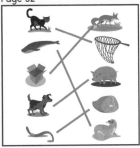

Page 33

Page 34

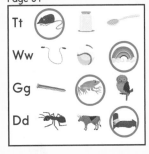

Page 35
1. n, 2. t, 3. l
4. m, 5. s, 6. g

Page 36

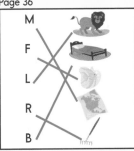

Page 37

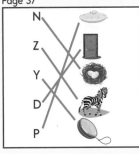

Page 38
1. h, 2. j, 3. v, 4. w, 5. qu

Page 39
1. g, 2. n, 3. s, 4. x, 5. t

Page 40
fan, map, rat, ham, bat

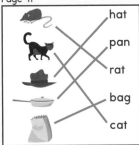

Page 41

hat

pan

rat

bag

cat

Page 42
nest, net, egg, dress, bed

Answers

Page 43

web
hen
ten
net
bed

Page 44
pig, zipper, fish, six, bib

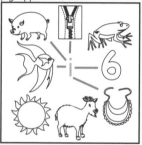

Page 45

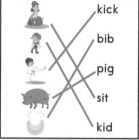

kick
bib
pig
sit
kid

Page 46
dog, lobster, mop, socks, box

Pages 47

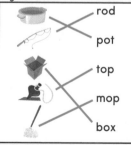

rod
pot
top
mop
box

Page 48
plug, drum, bus, duck, thumb

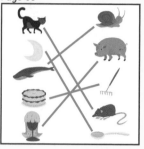

Page 49

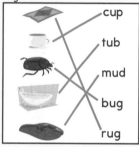

cup
tub
mud
bug
rug

Page 50
1. fat cat
2. bug hug

Page 51

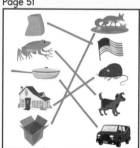

Page 52
1. man ran
2. fun run

Page 53

Page 54
1. big dig
2. pup cup

Page 55

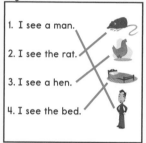

Page 56
1. I see a man.
2. I see the rat.
3. I see a hen.
4. I see the bed.

Pages 57–58
Each picture should match the sentence.

Page 59
1. I **see** the rat.
2. **I** see a man.
3. I see a **jet**.
4. I see **a** bed.

Page 60
1. I see a man and a cat.
2. The pig is wet.
3. It is a fox in a hat.
4. The rat is in the box.

Pages 61–62
Each picture should match the sentence.

Page 63
1. I see a cat **and** a dog.
2. The fox **is** red.
3. **It** is a big net.
4. The fan is **in** the den.

Page 64

a
e
i
o
u

Page 65
1. map, 2. bed, 3. web, 4. tub, 5. kick, 6. sock

Page 66

1. I see a wet dog in a tub.
2. It is a hen and a duck.
3. The red bug is in a net.
4. The pig is in the mud.

Page 67
1. **The** box is big and red.
2. I see a pan **and** a can.
3. The sun is big and **hot**.
4. **It** is ham in a can.

Page 68

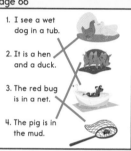

1. up
2. up
3. down
4. down

Page 69
1. The jet is **up**.
2. The man is **up**.
3. The jet is **down**.
4. The man is **down**.

Page 70

1. Mom said, "Go to bed."
2. The van can go up.
3. I see you in the bus.
4. Liz said "sit" to the dog.

Answers

Pages 71–72
Each picture should match the sentence.

Page 73
1. You **go** up in the jet.
2. I sit **down** in the jet.
3. You **said**, "It is fun."
4. The dog ran **to** the man.

Page 74

1. red
2. green
3. blue
4. yellow

Pages 75–76
Each picture should match the sentence.

Page 77
Suggestions:
yellow: school bus, sun, duck
red: fire engine, stop sign, apple
blue: whale, water, blueberry
green: tree, leaf, dragon

Page 78
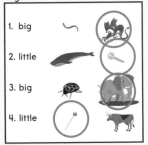

1. big
2. little
3. big
4. little

Page 79
1. The van is **big**.
2. The egg is **little**.
3. The top is **little**.
4. The bed is **big**.

Page 80
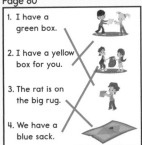

1. I have a green box.
2. I have a yellow box for you.
3. The rat is on the big rug.
4. We have a blue sack.

Pages 81–82
Each picture should match the sentence.

Page 83
1. We **have** a big van.
2. The mud is **on** the rug.
3. I have a job **for** you.
4. **We** see the yellow bus.

Page 84
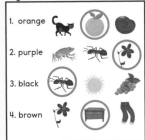

1. orange
2. purple
3. black
4. brown

Pages 85–86
Each picture should match the sentence.

Page 87
Suggestions:
orange: orange, goldfish
purple: flower, plum
black: ant, blackberry, road
brown: paper bag, mud, desk

Page 88

1. We look at the map.
2. She is not on the bus.
3. He is not sad.
4. We look for a bug.

Page 89
The picture should match the story.

Page 90
1. I **look** in the den for the dog.
2. **He** is a big man.
3. The duck is **not** purple.
4. She **is** a brown hen.

Page 91
The picture should match the story.

Page 92
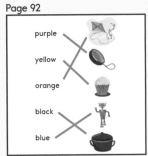

purple
yellow
orange
black
blue

Page 96
queen, cow, doctor, lion

Page 97
pig, dog, rat, hen

Page 98
man, cat, duck

Page 99
Pictures of a kid, a dog, a cat, and a rat

Page 100
house, barn, night

Page 101

Page 102

Page 103
Picture of a van on a road (on a hill)

Page 104
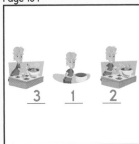

3   1   2

Page 105
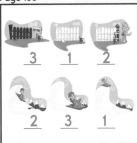

3   1   2
2   3   1

Page 106
Pictures should match the story sequence.

Page 107
Pictures should match the story sequence.

Page 108
Picture should show a solution to the problem.

Answers

Page 109

Page 110

Page 111
Pictures should match the story problem and solution.

Pages 112–113
Pictures should match the parts of the story.

Pages 114–115
Pictures should show the story events in order.

Page 116
unicorn, city, kite stuck in tree

Page 117